OUR
GRE★T
STATES

WHAT'S GREAT ABOUT
IOWA?

✸ Kristin Marciniak

LERNER PUBLICATIONS ✸ MINNEAPOLIS

CONTENTS

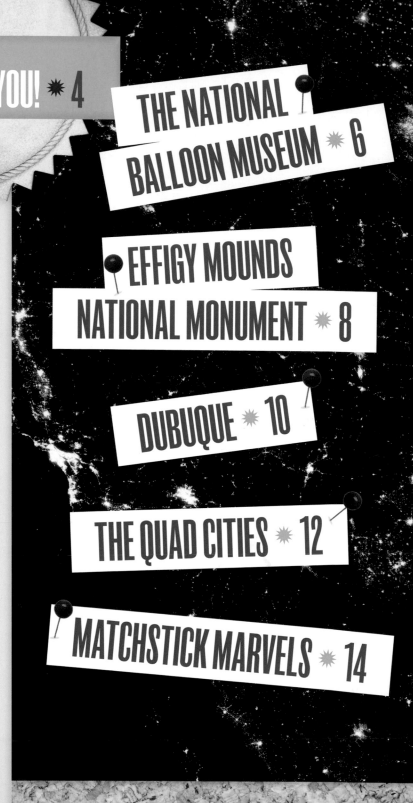
Copyright © 2015
by Lerner Publishing Group, Inc.

Content Consultant: Dr. Jeff Bremer, Assistant Professor of History, Iowa State University

Lerner Publications Company
A division of Lerner Publishing Group, Inc.
241 First Avenue North
Minneapolis, MN 55401 USA

For reading levels and more information, look up this title at www.lernerbooks.com.

Main body text set in ITC Franklin Gothic Std Book Condensed 12/15.
Typeface provided by Adobe Systems.

Library of Congress Cataloging-in-Publication Data

Marciniak, Kristin.
     What's great about Iowa? / by Kristin Marciniak.
         pages   cm. — (Our great states)
     Includes index.
     ISBN 978-1-4677-3868-2 (library binding : alkaline paper)
     ISBN 978-1-4677-6270-0 (eBook)
     1. Iowa—Juvenile literature. I. Title.
F621.3.M355 2015
977.7—dc23   2014018042

Manufactured in the United States of America
1 – PC – 12/31/14

IOWA Welcomes You!

Let's explore Iowa! This midwestern state is known for cornfields and farms. But Iowa is also home to big cities and small towns. Each has activities for the whole family. Hike through Effigy Mounds National Monument. Or catch a baseball game at Modern Woodmen Park. The park is along the mighty Mississippi River. Gobble up fresh ears of corn and pork sandwiches at the Iowa State Fair. From hot air balloons to statewide bike rides, there's something for everyone in Iowa. Read on to discover ten great things about the state!

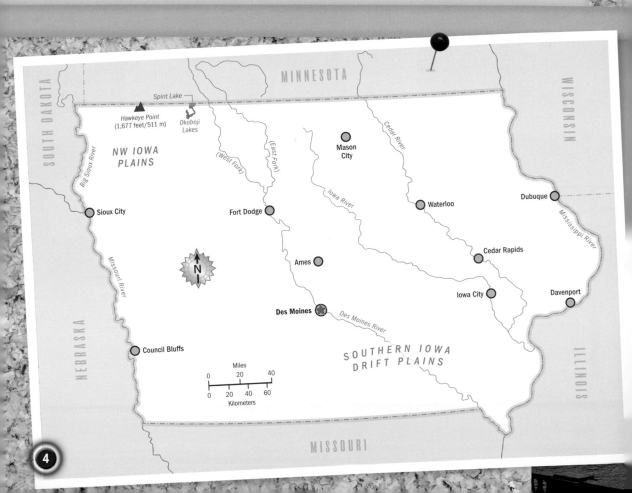

THE PEOPLE OF
IOWA
WELCOME YOU

Iowa

Fields of Opportunities

Explore Iowa's cities and all the places in between! Just turn the page to find out about the HAWKEYE STATE. >

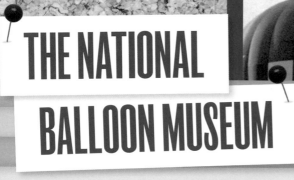

THE NATIONAL BALLOON MUSEUM

> One stop you won't want to miss on your trip to Iowa is in Indianola. Learn all about hot air balloons at the National Balloon Museum and US Ballooning Hall of Fame.

First, head to the Children's Learning Center. Climb inside a real balloon basket and have your photo taken. Pretend you're flying over green fields. Then practice flying a balloon in the computer game Hot Air Pilot. Keep your balloon in the air! After practicing, relax with a ballooning book in the Book Basket. This large wooden box is filled with cushions so you can get comfy as you read.

Visit in late July when Indianola hosts the National Balloon Classic. This nine-day festival has been taking place each year since 1989. You can listen to music or watch fireworks. If you're looking for more adventure, schedule a balloon ride. Sign up early because rides fill up fast.

THE IOWA CAUCUSES

Like many Iowans, people in Indianola play an important role in US politics. Every four years, Iowa holds the nation's first presidential caucuses. A caucus is when people gather to talk about political candidates. The Iowa caucuses are important. This is the first time Iowan voters share their opinions about the people who are running for president. It tells the rest of the country which candidate has a good chance of leading the United States.

Balloon baskets and paintings are just a few items you'll see in the National Balloon Museum.

EFFIGY MOUNDS
NATIONAL MONUMENT

> Make your next stop the Effigy Mounds National Monument in Harpers Ferry. These sacred American Indian mounds are near the Mississippi River valley. Twelve Woodland nations built them starting in 650 CE.

Start your visit at the visitor center. You'll want to watch a short video about the Mound Builders' ways. Head outside and choose a hiking trail. There are more than two hundred dirt mounds to see. Climb up one of the nearby steep hills and look down. From up high, you may see bear- or bird-shaped mounds. The birds and bears you see are called effigies. An effigy is something made to look like a person or an animal.

Hunt for the Great Bear Mound. This huge mound is 70 feet (21 meters) across and 137 feet (42 m) long. It is also 3 feet (1 m) high.

The Effigy Mounds (*above*) were used for ancient ceremonies. Explore exhibits and see ancient American Indian artifacts in the visitor center (*right*).

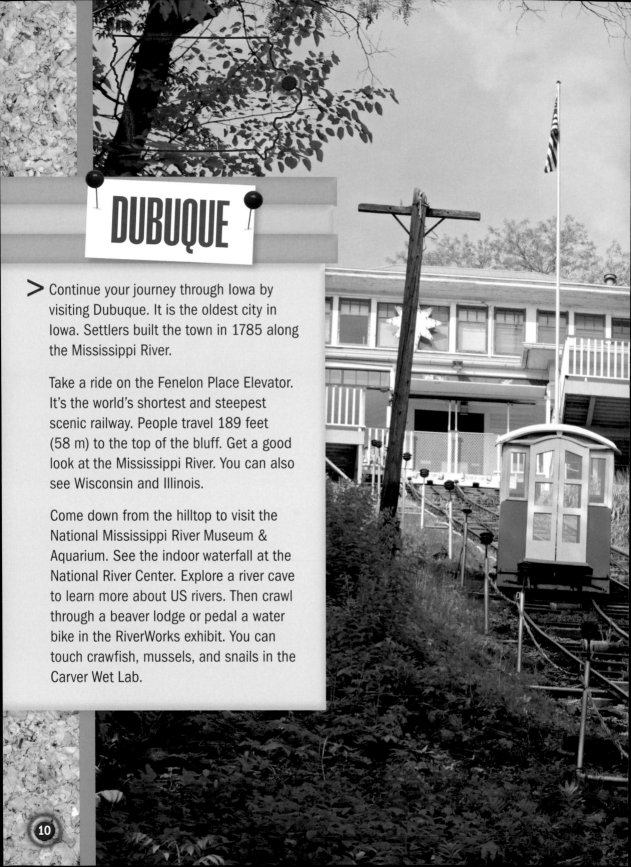

DUBUQUE

> Continue your journey through Iowa by visiting Dubuque. It is the oldest city in Iowa. Settlers built the town in 1785 along the Mississippi River.

Take a ride on the Fenelon Place Elevator. It's the world's shortest and steepest scenic railway. People travel 189 feet (58 m) to the top of the bluff. Get a good look at the Mississippi River. You can also see Wisconsin and Illinois.

Come down from the hilltop to visit the National Mississippi River Museum & Aquarium. See the indoor waterfall at the National River Center. Explore a river cave to learn more about US rivers. Then crawl through a beaver lodge or pedal a water bike in the RiverWorks exhibit. You can touch crawfish, mussels, and snails in the Carver Wet Lab.

EXPLORING THE MISSISSIPPI RIVER

The first Europeans visited Iowa in 1673. French king Louis XIV *(left)* sent explorers to find the river American Indians called *Messipi*, or "the Great Water." The explorers were to follow the river to the Pacific Ocean. They stopped in Iowa and wrote about its green, fertile land. As they continued on their journey, they realized the river emptied into the Gulf of Mexico, not the Pacific Ocean.

See catfish in one of the National Mississippi River Museum's twelve aquariums.

THE QUAD CITIES

> A fun place to explore in Iowa is the Quad Cities area. Despite its name, the area is actually made up of five cities, not four. Bettendorf and Davenport are in Iowa. Moline, East Moline, and Rock Island are in Illinois. The Mississippi River separates the two states and the Quad Cities.

Play the day away at the Family Museum in Bettendorf. You'll harvest corn, collect eggs, and pick apples at the George's Farm exhibit. Climb around in Farmer George's tree house. Then practice being a postal carrier, a veterinarian, or a firefighter in the Fox Hollow exhibit. Get your hands wet at Lil 'Ssippi River Valley. Move boats down the 28-foot-long (8.5 m) waterplay table.

Stop at Modern Woodmen Park in Davenport. It is home to the Quad Cities River Bandits, a minor-league baseball team. Munch on your favorite ballpark snacks while you cheer on the home team!

Skip across kid-sized models of three local bridges at the Family Museum.

RISING WATERS

Most cities along the Mississippi River are protected from flooding by levees. These cement walls rise several feet above the riverbank. They keep floodwaters from reaching homes and businesses. Davenport battled more than twelve floods between 1960 and 2011. Property was destroyed. A few people even died. The city now has a small levee. It protects the water company building.

MATCHSTICK MARVELS

> The city of Gladbrook has a population of about 934 people. But this tiny town is home to some really big art. You'll want to visit the Matchstick Marvels Tourist Center to see it. All the art is built out of matchsticks.

Patrick Acton *(far right)* is a local artist. He uses matchsticks and wood glue to build scale models of ships, space shuttles, and castles. Each matchstick is 2 inches (5 centimeters) long. It takes a lot of matchsticks to build a model. Some models take years to complete. Check out Acton's work at the Matchstick Marvels museum.

Study the details on the matchstick Notre Dame. It is a model of a church in Paris, France. The model was built with 298,000 matchsticks. Make sure to see the 12-foot-long (3.7 m) US Capitol. The model of this building even lights up!

You'll see a model of the *Challenger* space shuttle at the Matchstick Marvels museum.

PELLA

> There's no place quite like Pella. This central Iowa city is proud of its Dutch heritage. You may feel as if you're touring Holland, not Iowa. The best time to visit Pella is during Tulip Time. It takes place during the first weekend in May. This festival celebrates the eighty thousand tulips that bloom in Pella each year. Locals dress in colorful Dutch clothing, including wooden shoes. Try on a pair and march in the Tulip Time parades.

Pella is also home to the Vermeer Mill. It is 124 feet (38 m) tall. Explore the Historical Village next to the mill. These twenty buildings show what Pella was like from the 1800s to the 1900s.

The Vermeer Mill is the tallest working windmill in the United States.

After Pella's Tulip Time parades, walk through the beautiful tulip gardens.

LIVING HISTORY FARMS

> Iowa is known for farming. Get your hands dirty at Living History Farms in Urbandale. This outdoor museum is made up of three working farms and an old-fashioned town.

Start your visit at the 1700 Ioway Indian Farm. You'll learn the roles of Ioway women and men in the 1700s. Help prepare and cook stew over an open fire. Then walk through an Ioway house.

Next, jump ahead 150 years to the 1850 Pioneer Farm. Help saw wood, harvest wheat, and visit the calves and lambs. Then see what a difference fifty years make at the 1900 Horse-Powered Farm. Pump water, feed the pigs, and use historic tools to crack and shell corn.

End your day at the 1875 Town of Walnut Hill. See actors dressed in period clothing from the 1800s. Then pick up a souvenir at the general store.

FARMING: THEN AND NOW

In 1900, US farms employed 41 percent of workers. More than one hundred years later, only 2 percent of people work on farms. Better farming technology is one of the reasons for this big drop. Iowa farmers used to depend on horses to power tools such as plows. Now they use gas-powered machines that can plow, plant, and harvest huge fields in a short period of time.

POST OFFICE

Walnut Hill, Iowa

STORE

GOODS

CINES

DUCE

MATTHIAS ☙ BLACKSMITH

Watch the blacksmith
work in Walnut Hill.

19

THE IOWA STATE FAIR

> More than one million people come to Des Moines each year for the Iowa State Fair. It is the largest event in the state, lasting eleven days in August. Start your day exploring the fairgrounds on the AgVenture Discovery Trail. This scavenger hunt will take you past animals and crops. Visit all eleven stops on your map, and then turn it in for a prize.

August in Iowa can get pretty warm. Cool down with the life-size butter cow. The statue is made from 600 pounds (272 kilograms) of real butter. It is kept in a 40°F (4°C) cooler. Or check out the Fun Forest and Pella Plaza. These areas have shady trees, playground equipment, and fountains to play in.

Getting hungry? The Iowa State Fair is famous for food on a stick. Choose from sixty types, including pickles, pork chops, and even salad.

Wrap up your day with a few carnival rides and games. Take a ride down the giant slide, or see the Des Moines skyline from the double Ferris wheel.

Take a ride on the swings or try a classic fair food, such as the corn dog, at the Iowa State Fair.

CORN DOGS

IOWA GREAT LAKES

> Iowa is completely landlocked. This means there is land on all or most of the state's sides. Even so, there are plenty of beaches for summertime fun. Spend a couple of days at the Iowa Great Lakes in the northwestern corner of the state. Spirit Lake is the largest of the nine lakes. Looking for adventure? Try waterskiing or wakeboarding.

Get back on dry land and head to the Dickinson County Nature Center in Okoboji. Wander through the butterfly house. Play in the rock sculpture area. Hike the nature trails to the one-room schoolhouse. It was built more than one hundred years ago!

Round out your trip at Arnolds Park Amusement Park. Race go-carts and brave the wooden roller coaster. Ride to the top of the 63-foot (19 m) Ferris wheel. Enjoy the beautiful view of the lakes.

Stretch your muscles in a kayak on one of Iowa's Great Lakes.

IOWA'S LAND

Many people assume Iowa is flat. It's true that it has no mountains, but the state is actually sloped. The eastern part of the state, along the Mississippi River, is the low end. The terrain slopes upward more than 1,000 feet (305 m) as you move northwest toward the Iowa Great Lakes.

STATEWIDE BIKE RIDE

> One of the best ways to see Iowa is from a bicycle. You can do just that during RAGBRAI. The Register's Annual Great Bicycle Ride Across Iowa has been around since 1973. It's the oldest, largest, and longest cycling event in the world.

RAGBRAI takes place during the last full week of July. There is a different route each year. It always starts in western Iowa on the Missouri River. It ends in eastern Iowa on the Mississippi River. Bikers pedal from town to town during the day.

You need to register in advance to be one of RAGBRAI's ten thousand riders. Riders under the age of eighteen will need to sign up with a parent or a guardian. Participate for all seven days or for just one leg of the trip. If you don't want to ride, you can cheer on cyclists from all around the world. RAGBRAI is the best way to see Iowa—one small town at a time.

Some RAGBRAI bikers camp in tents or sleep in an RV for the night.

YOUR TOP TEN!

Now that you've read about ten awesome things to see and do in Iowa, think about what your Iowa top ten list would include. What would you like to see if you visited the state? What would you like to do there? What would you be most excited about if you were planning an Iowa vacation? These are all questions to consider as you think about your own top ten. Make your list on a separate sheet of paper. You can even turn your list into a book and illustrate it with drawings or pictures from the Internet or magazines.

IOWA BY MAP

Visit www.lerneresource.com to learn more about the state flag of Iowa.

> MAP KEY

- ⬟ Capital city
- ⭘ City
- ◉ Point of interest
- ▲ Highest elevation
- –·– State border
- —— RAGBRAI (2014 route)

IOWA

(West Fork)

Spirit Lake

SOUTH DAKOTA

Hawkeye Point
(1,677 feet/511 m) ▲

Okoboji
Lakes ◉

Dickinson
County
Nature Center
(Okoboji)

NW
IOWA
PLAINS

Big Sioux River

⭘ Sioux City

N

Missouri River

NEBRASKA

◉ Council Bluffs

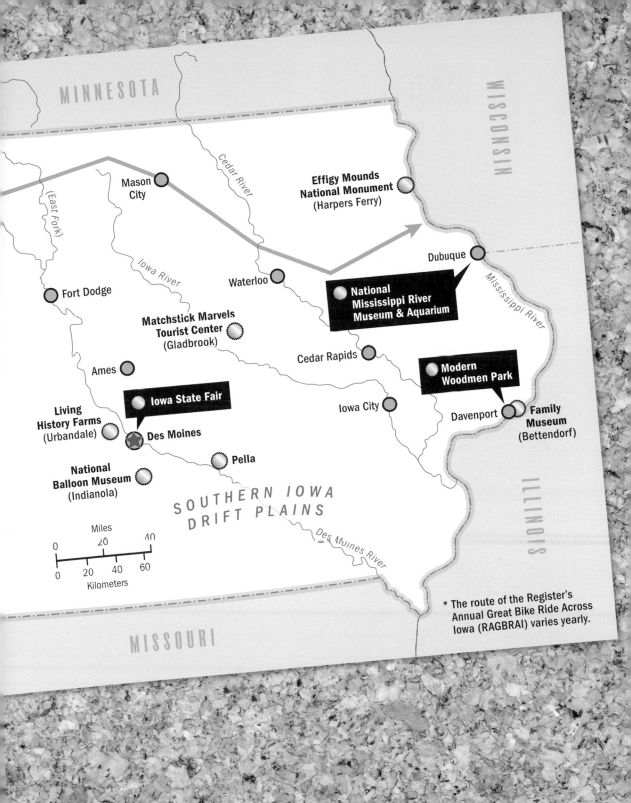

MINNESOTA

WISCONSIN

(East Fork)

Mason City

Cedar River

Effigy Mounds
National Monument
(Harpers Ferry)

Dubuque

Mississippi River

Iowa River

Fort Dodge

Waterloo

**National
Mississippi River
Museum & Aquarium**

Matchstick Marvels
Tourist Center
(Gladbrook)

Cedar Rapids

**Modern
Woodmen Park**

Ames

Iowa State Fair

Iowa City

Davenport

**Family
Museum**
(Bettendorf)

Living
History Farms
(Urbandale)

Des Moines

Pella

National
Balloon Museum
(Indianola)

SOUTHERN IOWA
DRIFT PLAINS

Des Moines River

ILLINOIS

Miles
0   20   40
0   20   40   60
Kilometers

* The route of the Register's
Annual Great Bike Ride Across
Iowa (RAGBRAI) varies yearly.

MISSOURI

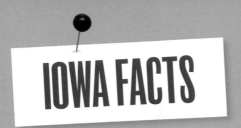

IOWA FACTS

NICKNAME: The Hawkeye State

SONG: "The Song of Iowa" by S. H. M. Byers

MOTTO: "Our liberties we prize and our rights we will maintain."

> **FLOWER:** wild rose

TREE: oak

> **BIRD:** American goldfinch

DATE AND RANK OF STATEHOOD: December 28, 1846; the 29th state

> **CAPITAL:** Des Moines

AREA: 56,273 square miles (145,746 sq. km)

AVERAGE JANUARY TEMPERATURE: 19°F (–7°C)

AVERAGE JULY TEMPERATURE: 75°F (24°C)

POPULATION AND RANK: 3,046,355; 30th (2013)

MAJOR CITIES AND POPULATIONS: Des Moines (203,433), Cedar Rapids (126,326), Davenport (99,685), Sioux City (82,684), Waterloo (68,406)

NUMBER OF US CONGRESS MEMBERS: 4 representatives, 2 senators

NUMBER OF ELECTORAL VOTES: 6

NATURAL RESOURCES: crushed limestone, gypsum, sands, gravel, clay and shale

> **AGRICULTURAL PRODUCTS:** beef cattle, corn, eggs, hogs, milk, soybeans

MANUFACTURED GOODS: chemicals, computer and electronic parts, food products, machinery, plastic and rubber products

STATE HOLIDAYS AND CELEBRATIONS: Iowa State Fair

GLOSSARY

fertile: able to produce many plants or crops

heritage: something learned from the past

landlocked: surrounded or nearly surrounded by land

leg: a portion of a trip

levee: a bank built along a river to prevent flooding

mound: a small hill or heap of dirt or stones

sacred: holy or religious

scale: size in comparison

souvenir: something that serves as a reminder

LERNER

SOURCE

Expand learning beyond the printed book. Download free, complementary educational resources for this book from our website, www.lernerresource.com.

FURTHER INFORMATION

Dickinson County Nature Center Osprey Camera
http://dickinsoncountyconservationboard.com/osprey-camera
Watch the streaming video of ospreys and their baby chicks during the spring and summer.

Higgins, Nadia. *What's Great about Minnesota?* Minneapolis: Lerner Publications, 2015. Learn more about Iowa's neighboring state Minnesota.

Lusted, Marcia Amidon. *Iowa: The Hawkeye State*. New York: PowerKids Press, 2010. Iowa comes to life in this book about the state's history, economy, people, and places.

Matchstick Marvels
http://www.matchstickmarvels.com
This site includes photos and details about every model matchstick artist Patrick Acton has ever made, including those that are no longer on-site.

Miller, Dean, and Jeffrey Talbot. *Iowa*. New York: Cavendish Square Publishing, 2014. Get the scoop on Iowa's history, people, and culture while you cook a local dish and create an Iowa-themed craft.

Travel Iowa
http://www.traveliowa.com
Start your vacation planning on Iowa's official tourism website. From places to stay to things to do, it's all covered right here.

INDEX

PHOTO ACKNOWLEDGMENTS

The images in this book are used with the permission of: © MaxyM/Shutterstock Images, p. 1; NASA, pp. 2–3; © Laura Westlund/Independent Picture Service, pp. 4, 26–27; © Henryk Sadura/Shutterstock Images, pp. 4–5; © Spirit of America/Shutterstock Images, pp. 5, 8–9; © Michael Rolands/Shutterstock Images, pp. 6–7; © Robert Cross/MCT/Newscom, pp. 7 (bottom), 18–19; © Getty Images/Thinkstock, p. 7 (top); © Clint Farlinger/Alamy, p. 9; © Jamie & Judy Wild Danita Delimont Photography/Newscom, pp. 10–11; © Richard Wong/Alamy, p. 11 (bottom); Library of Congress, pp. 11 (top) (LC-USZ62-124397), 13 (bottom) (LC-DIG-highsm-04394), 18 (LC-USF34-028087-D), 29 (bottom right) (LC-DIG-highsm-15231); © David Welker/Four Seam Images/AP Images, pp. 12–13; © Zuma Press, Inc./Alamy, p. 13 (top); © CB2/ZOB/WENN/Newscom, pp. 14–15; © Splash News/Newscom, p. 14; © Jerry Hopman/Thinkstock, p. 16; © Elaine McDonald/Thinkstock, pp. 16–17, 17; © George and Monserrate Schwartz/Alamy, p. 19; © Madeleine Openshaw/Shutterstock Images, pp. 20–21; © Matthew Ennis/Shutterstock Images, p. 21 (left); © Suzanne Tucker/Shutterstock Images, p. 21 (right); © Jesse Kunerth/Shutterstock Images, pp. 22–23; © lightpoet/Shutterstock Images, p. 23 (top); © Igor Kovalenko/Shutterstock Images, p. 23 (bottom); © Kevin E. Schmidt/Zuma Press/Newscom, pp. 24–25; © Monkey Business Images/Shutterstock Images, p. 25; © nicoolay/iStockphoto, p. 26; © Bikeworldtravel/Shutterstock Images, p. 29 (top right); © Al Mueller/Shutterstock Images, p. 29 (top left); © Paul Orr/Shutterstock Images, p. 29 (bottom left).

Cover: AP Photo/Mike Burley (RAGBRAI); © iStockphoto.com/Elaine McDonald (tulips); © olgakr/iStock/Thinkstock (corn); © Laura Westlund/Independent Picture Service (map); © iStockphoto.com/fpm (seal); © iStockphoto.com/vicm (pushpins); © iStockphoto.com/benz190 (corkboard).